YOUR RICH LIFE

YOUR RICH LIFE

A Human Approach to Investment and Building the Wealth of Your Dreams

JONATHAN SATOVSKY

△ SATOVSKY™
ASSET MANAGEMENT

YOUR RICH LIFE

*A Human Approach to Investment and
Building the Wealth of Your Dreams*

ISBN   978-1-5445-0277-9 *Paperback*
          978-1-5445-0278-6 *Ebook*

CONTENTS

INTRODUCTION

YOUR OWN WORST ENEMY

The investor's chief problem—and even his worst enemy—is likely to be himself.

BENJAMIN GRAHAM, *THE INTELLIGENT INVESTOR*

In the investing world, there's an intense amount of focus on market fluctuations that cost investors money. Less attention is paid to a far more pressing reason for widespread losses: the *Behavior Gap*, a term coined by the *New York Times* sketch artist and former financial planner Carl Richards. The Behavior Gap describes the difference between the higher returns that investors might potentially earn, and the lower returns they actually do earn because of their own behavior. This generally occurs due to emotional reactions causing shorter holding periods, which often results in buying at highs (euphoric moments) and selling at lows (moments of despair or extreme pessimism about the future).

Below is Carl's cocktail napkin sketch illustrating this point.

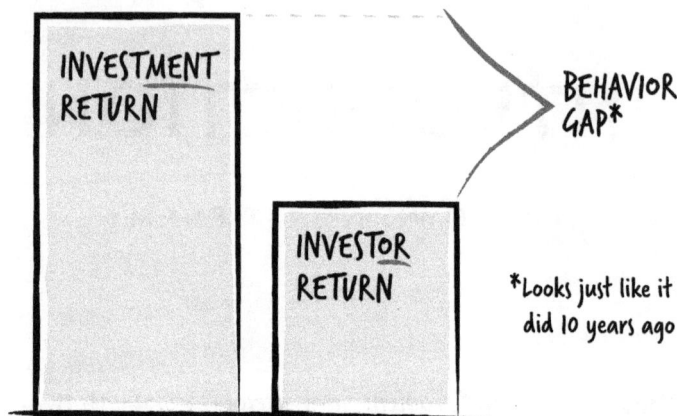

What do I mean by bad behavior? In a nutshell, the average holding period for investments in our society has been shrinking dramatically.

In his book *Enough: True Measure of Money, Business, and Life*, the investor and philanthropist John Bogle points out that in 1951, the average holding period for fund investors was about sixteen years. Today, however, that holding period averages about four years or less. And to make matters worse, oftentimes, fund investors don't trade very successfully.

Why is this? It's usually because they are chasing good performance and abandoning ship at the first sign of bad performance. Thus, the returns investors actually walked away with (the asset-weighted returns) have trailed the annualized, time-weighted returns reported by the funds themselves by a gap Bogle estimates at an astonishing 2.7 percent per year.

Today, having tracked data internally as well as externally for hundreds of individuals and institutional portfolios and investors, I can confirm that the Behavior Gap is real[1]—and it's a problem that many who work outside of the financial industry aren't even aware of. Candidly, I'm not so sure those inside the industry are aware of it either and perhaps could be exacerbating it for their own perceived career survival.

THROW OUT THE SHORT-TERM MONEY MINDSET

This short-term investment mindset is not a recipe for success over a lifetime. It's generally understood in the finance world that, over time, stocks (ownership interest in businesses) outperform bonds (loans to governments, businesses, or individuals), which in turn outperform cash. It follows that the biggest potential returns come

---

1   Since 2007, Satovsky Asset Management has utilized a technology tool called Black Diamond Reporting Software, a third-party platform that provides automated data aggregation and reconciliation of clients' financial data. It also tracks details down to the dollar-weighted and time-weighted returns. After a decade of utilizing this reporting tool, it is common for the dollar-weighted returns to be lower than the time-weighted returns (investor returns lower than investment returns). It makes total sense. When investors see their portfolios doing well, they are inclined to add to them. When they are not, they are inclined to sell, or at least they fail to seize the bargain opportunity by buying more.

from holding stocks. Evidence-based research has also shown that small company stocks outperform larger company stocks, and that you can maximize your returns further by focusing on a value orientation (i.e., buying something cheap) and focusing on profitable businesses.

This philosophy has been proven to work around the world—not all the time, granted, but with a high probability of success if these kinds of investments are held over the long term.

Historical Performance of Premiums over Rolling Periods (US Markets)

MARKET beat T-BILLS (Jul 1926–Dec 2017)

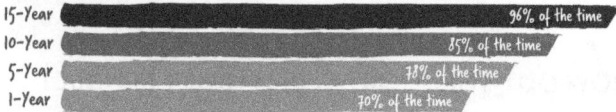

15-Year	96% of the time
10-Year	85% of the time
5-Year	78% of the time
1-Year	70% of the time

VALUE beat GROWTH (Jul 1926–Dec 2017)

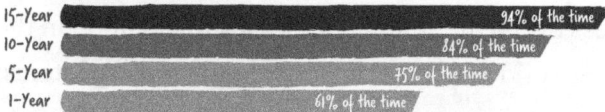

15-Year	94% of the time
10-Year	84% of the time
5-Year	75% of the time
1-Year	61% of the time

SMALL beat LARGE (June 1927–Dec 2017)

15-Year	85% of the time
10-Year	72% of the time
5-Year	64% of the time
1-Year	57% of the time

HIGH PROFITABILITY beat LOW PROFITABILITY (Jul 1963–Dec 2017)

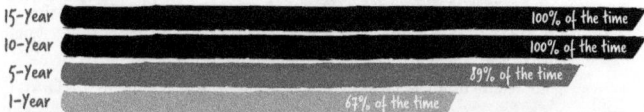

15-Year	100% of the time
10-Year	100% of the time
5-Year	89% of the time
1-Year	67% of the time

Information provided by Dimensional Fund Advisors LP. In US dollars. 1. Profitability is a measure of current profitability, based on information from individual companies' income statements, scaled by book. Based on rolling annualized returns using monthly data. Rolling multiyear periods overlap and are not independent. "One-Month Treasury Bills" is the IA SBBI US 30 Day TBill TR USD, provided by Ibbotson Associates via Morningstar Direct. Dimensional Index data compiled by Dimensional. FAMA/French data provided by FAMA/French. S&P data copyright 2018 S&P Dow Jones Indices LLC, a division of S&P Global. All rights reserved. Indices are not available for direct investment. Past performance is not a guarantee of future results. Eugene Fama and Ken French are members of the Board of Directors of the general partner of, and provide consulting services to, Dimensional Fund Advisors LP. Index descriptions available upon request.

But owing to our instant-gratification culture, patience and long holding periods are no longer the norm. I've witnessed and documented that by taking shorter evaluation periods of about three years investors routinely see their investments underperform by 1 percent to 6 percent annually over what they could have made holding the same assets for a decade. Here is a wonderful visual image that provides estimates of the Behavioral Gap.[2]

Estimate of the Behavior Gap

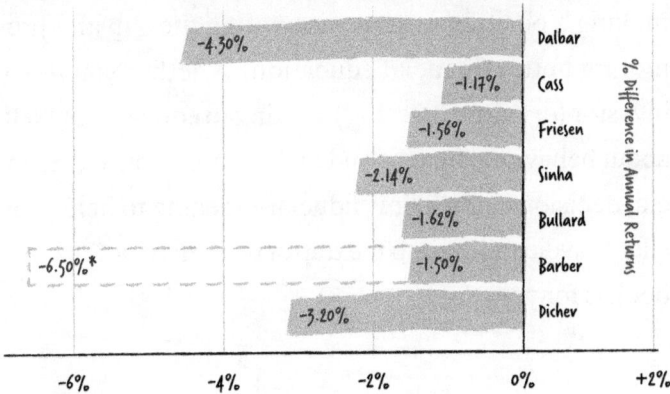

	% Difference in Annual Returns
-4.30%	Dalbar
-1.17%	Cass
-1.56%	Friesen
-2.14%	Sinha
-1.62%	Bullard
-6.50%* / -1.50%	Barber
-3.20%	Dichev

-6%   -4%   -2%   0%   +2%

See reference for links to published results and methodologies. *Given for the most actively trading investors in sample.

A number of academic studies have similarly estimated the cost of the Behavior Gap. I've made it my personal goal to eliminate this gap from the portfolios of my clients—and **my hope is that discussion can help avoid**

---

2   Patrick Burns, "Betterment's Quest for Behavior Gap Zero," Betterment, accessed April 11, 2019. Financial technology provider Betterment documents their own quest for Behavioral Gap zero, which they periodically update.

https://www.betterment.com/resources/betterments-quest-behavior-gap-zero

the pitfalls now, for you, my readers—as much as possible.

It's a shame that we don't learn basic financial literacy as part of our high school curricula. This means that most people learn to manage (or mismanage) their wealth through experience, which boils down to trial and error, leading to problems like the Behavior Gap.

That's why I decided to write this book—in the hopes of making a positive dent in eliminating the gap and promoting better financial education. Whether you're an investor (or future investor!) seeking to educate yourself about behavioral finance and make more informed financial decisions, or a fellow fiduciary seeking to help your clients avoid falling into the trap of the Behavior Gap, this book is for you.

GUIDE TO A MORE PROSPEROUS FUTURE

Now let me tell you a little about myself.

My name is Jonathan Satovsky, and I am the founder and CEO of Satovsky Asset Management, LLC (SAM), an independent Registered Investment Advisory firm on Madison Avenue in New York City. We advise institutions and multigenerational families around the world with assets and balance sheets in excess of two billion dollars.

We have discretionary responsibility for managing more than one-half-billion dollars of those assets.

Previously, I spent thirteen years at American Express Financial Advisors (now Ameriprise) as one of the youngest advisors on the Chairman's Advisory Council, representing the top 1 percent of the firm. In 2007, I started an independent firm, becoming one of the top ten American Express advisors in the country, before finally deciding it was time for a new challenge. That's when I struck out on my own.

Our boutique firm is in the advice business. We seek to build lifetime relationships with our clients—both individuals and institutions. Most of our time is spent working with friends and family to help navigate the Rubik's Cube of financial planning, investing, and behavioral decisions to provide for a lifetime of financial security. We have built a 98 percent retention rate over two decades.

Each day, I am inspired to raise my own game by continually seeking to create new and lasting ways to help clients make confident, informed decisions that make a positive impact beyond just dollars and cents. What we work toward with our clients, ultimately, is a transformative mindset shift away from scarcity thinking and toward abundance and tranquility. *That's* how we help them—and ourselves—to achieve the resilient, long-term strategy mindset needed to stay the course, close the Behavior Gap, and get the most from our investments.

I run more than just a business. This is personal for me.

My own interest in the field of personal finance began at twelve years old when my parents got divorced. After my parents split up, I lived with my mother, and I saw firsthand how financially vulnerable she had become by going back to work as a single mom. Since then, I've been making calculated personal decisions to try to be as financially independent as possible to minimize this vulnerability—for myself and for the people I care about.

The crux of much of my advice to others is meant to enable them to be financially independent and self-sufficient with sustainable finances. I'm passionate about sharing the wealth of knowledge I've accumulated and the creative workarounds I've developed over the years. I continue to learn and grow each day.

It's in my heart and soul to help people improve their financial lives and outlooks. That's why I do what I do, and it's why I wrote this book.

HOW TO GET THE MOST OUT OF THIS BOOK

As I mentioned above, I've written this book with a little

something for everyone—whether you're a new or veteran investor, or a fellow professional in the financial industry. In brief, here's what I'll be covering in the chapters to come.

The Road to Financial Well-Being. For most of us, we learn basic finance as we go through life—or sometimes not at all. Here I lay out the three primary aspects of financial literacy that everyone should know. I'll also cover useful groundwork for understanding how investments work, practical guidelines for financial stability, and some thoughts on how the financial industry works from a consumer perspective.

A Crash Course in Behavioral Finance. Here I lay out more advanced principles fundamental to behavioral finance. Once you understand best practices and potential pitfalls along the way, you'll be better equipped to practice the former and avoid the latter.

Quest for an Abundant Life. Finally, I share my vision for a more financially prosperous future, despite the doom-and-gloom tidings we see every day when we turn on the news. Drawing on the wisdom of financial titans like Warren Buffett, I lay out how to adopt and promote the necessary mindset of resilient calm required in order to get the best from a long-term financial strategy for success.

Appendix: For Financial Professionals: Philosophy and Principles. As a financial professional, how can I best help my clients to be successful in their long-term investing, financial, and life goals? In this appendix, geared toward my fellow fiduciaries, I share my own thoughts, as well as wisdom from my mentors, on how we can best serve our clients and the greater community.

AN ABUNDANT FUTURE

When I was a kid, I loved the *Choose Your Own Adventure* books, because they allowed me to choose the path that most appealed to me. Life is and *should* be a "choose your own adventure" story. Your money is what gives you the power to write that adventure yourself instead of following a script meant for someone else.

Whatever financial freedom means for you—or your clients—my goal is to empower you with the knowledge you need to get there. Before you know it, you'll be empowered to change your life and your future—starting right now.

Chapter One

THE ROAD TO FINANCIAL WELL-BEING

It is not so very important for a person to learn facts. For that he does not really need college. He can learn them from books. The value of an education in a liberal arts college is not the learning of many facts, but the training of the mind to think something that cannot be learned from textbooks.

ALBERT EINSTEIN

Did you know there's a reported $6.6 trillion anticipated shortage in people's retirement funds here in the United States? In fact, 63 percent of retirees are dependent on Social Security, friends, and charity for financial survival, according to The Motley Fool.[3] Even people who accumulate tremendous riches have difficulty with money. Sixty percent of NBA players go broke five years after they retire, 78 percent of NFL players are bankrupt two years after retirement, and 30 percent of lottery winners likewise run out of money in short order.[4]

Generations that inherit wealth are burdened in just three generations with "shirtsleeves to shirtsleeves" challenges.[5] In other words, one entrepreneur or wealth creator works hard to accumulate riches, leading to his or her second generation becoming more educated and increasing the family's standard of living. But then, the third generation comes along and generally blows it all. This cycle typically starts all over by the fifth generation.

So, what's the solution to all of these problems?

Some would say simple financial literacy, but there's more than meets the eye when it comes to learning to successfully manage your finances to achieve true independence.

---

3   Matthew Frankel, "20 Retirement Stats That Will Blow You Away," The Motley Fool, January 26, 2016, https://www.fool.com/retirement/general/2016/01/26/20-retirement-stats-that-will-blow-you-away.aspx.

4   Pablo S. Torre, "How (and Why) Athletes Go Broke," *Sports Illustrated*, March 22, 2009, https://www.si.com/vault/2009/03/23/105789480/how-and-why-athletes-go-broke.

5   "To Have and to Hold, Special Report," *The Economist*, June 14, 2001, https://www.economist.com/node/654077.

Since we don't learn this in school—though we *should*—we have to learn it somewhere else, which means, unfortunately, most of us pick this stuff up through the mistakes we make along the way. That is, if we're wise enough to learn from them. And that's really the key here—we have to be in a position to actually make good on what we learn.

Most financial advisors market themselves by boasting that they outperform the market, or "deliver alpha." The reality is that after fees, taxes, and then investor behavior, almost no one does. In fact, as I see it, the job of a responsible fiduciary isn't to *outperform* the market, but to do everything in our power to close the Behavior Gap and help clients achieve their long-term financial goals.

In this chapter, we'll cover some foundational basics of how to become financially literate about your own current and future finances, as well as some common sense guidelines for how to get the best out of your financial and investment strategy.

THE BASICS: WHAT YOU NEED TO KNOW

My view of how to best help clients understand financial literacy is to keep it as simple as possible. We start with coming to an understanding of not just what our clients' current finances are like, but what their goals are. And I don't just mean their financial goals, but rather what it is they want out of life. Then, we reverse engineer those goals to create a financial strategy that will take the client from *here* to *there* on a comfortable route.

To make that strategy work, I have to convince my clients of an odd truth: our decision-making and mindset when it comes to finances often has very little to do with money. Instead, our thinking is often rooted in a story that was created during childhood—stories we now, as adults, take for granted as just the way things are. My own story was informed by my parents' divorce and my burning desire to be financially independent rather than vulnerably dependent.

This holistic approach to personal finance has evolved into a management process in which I see myself rather like a family doctor for my clients' finances. Step one is to take an inventory, rather like initial "bloodwork" on someone's financial life. This inventory has three basic components.

STEP 1: BALANCE SHEET

A balance sheet is a snapshot of a person's financial assets (what you own) and liabilities (what you owe) at a given moment in time. Though this sounds simple, for many prospective clients I've discovered that it is often the first time in their lives that they have gone through this exercise (and many of these people are in their fifties or older.) I recommend reviewing—and as needed, updating—your balance sheet at least annually to get a handle on where you stand and to help in the decision-making process. Think of this process like getting your annual preventative care checkup with your doctor—only here, you're monitoring your financial health and well-being.

STEP 2: CASH FLOW

A cash flow statement reviews all your sources of income and subtracts fixed and variable expenses, resulting in a clear picture of how much net income is actually flowing in. Sample sources include employment or self-employment income, passive revenue sources from investments, Social Security, and pension income. Expenses can include fixed expenses for housing (recommended to be kept at a maximum of 28 percent to 33 percent of income), variable lifestyle expenses, philanthropic giving (a recommended 10 percent of income), savings into non-retirement and retirement accounts, and income taxes. The net difference between total income and total expenses reflects your free cash flow.

STEP 3: GOALS

Once an inventory has been taken on your financials, with such necessary supporting documents as tax returns, wills/trusts, insurance policies, investment statements, and employee benefits, the next step is a holistic examination of your goals and the mindset needed to achieve these.

As I've said, goal setting is one thing, but following through is a difficult process for most. Developing good habits is absolutely critical to increasing the probability of lifetime financial success and sustainability.

Bottom line, we're all human, and each of us is affected by behavioral biases. That's why cultivating emotional intelligence and the right mindset are so important, on top of educating ourselves about essential financial basics.

In my line of work, I've learned I can share all the requisite facts about financial literacy, but what really makes a difference in how people make use of the information available to them boils down to four things.

1. **Mindset.** The most successful people I work with learn to see investing and building wealth as a lifelong process. They avoid anxious, short-term decision-making. They assume a world of abundance, not scarcity—an attitude and frame for decision-making that's healthier for both your wealth and health. I have many clients in their eighties and nineties who, like Warren Buffett, have lived through the Great

Depression, World War II, booms and busts. They share a generational mindset of owning something for a lifetime, through the ups and downs, and understand that growth isn't in a straight line.

2. **Structure.** In order to allow for longer-term thinking, it is important to understand your own balance sheet and future cash flow needs. Life doesn't always go as expected, so tinkering is ongoing, but if you can create a fundamental structure for financial planning that makes intellectual sense to you, you will reduce finance-related stress and pave the way to a wealthier and healthier life. You also have to understand your own temperament so that you can develop a plan you can live with while the market fluctuates. Just the other day, markets took a dive, and I went through a visual of the daily losses to our conservative versus aggressive clients. The losses on the aggressive portfolios would have our conservative clients in total panic, leading inevitably to poor short-term decision-making.

3. **Self-Discipline.** Every day, amazing new opportunities cross our desk; or worse, we witness others getting rich off of investments we haven't made. The most successful investors don't let themselves be seduced or distracted from their plans. They also ignore the constant inflow of negative news predicting disaster

around every corner, which leads so many others to either paralysis or impulse.

The best example I can recall of someone with unshakeable discipline of conviction isn't even in finance, he's in sports: John Beilein, the men's basketball coach at the University of Michigan, my alma mater. He's known for his rigid recruiting practices, which have made it difficult for him to sign top talent despite taking his team to the national championship title game in 2013 and 2018. He's constantly criticized for not landing the five-star recruits that other big schools sign routinely—and yet, the naysayers can only cut so deep because he's nevertheless built one of the most competitive teams in college basketball. He develops players with a flexible, yet disciplined, process that supports self-sacrifice for the team. When Beilein got to Michigan in 2007, it had been in a decade-long NCAA tournament drought. But by the second half of his fourth season, things were turning around. Since 2011, Michigan has won 70 percent of its games, averaging twenty-five wins per season. In those seven years, this program has four Sweet 16, two Elite Eight, two Final Four, and two national title game appearances, two Big Ten regular season titles, two Big Ten Tournament titles and seven NBA draft picks.[6] Whatever he's doing, it's working. During the process of writing this book, he's taken on the challenge to coach in the NBA and has hired the first woman's assistant coach in NBA history.

4. **Optimism.** The future is always better than people think, and the more you believe that, the easier it becomes to view setbacks as learning opportunities. There are no screwups, only AFGOs (*another f$!%ing growth opportunity*). This mindset is not only a healthier and wealthier way to live, it helps you embrace the future with resilience and the excitement of limitless possibility. Every failure then sets the stage for a bigger and better future.

You've got to think like a baseball player. The Major League Baseball batting averages from 1901 through 2017 have been a paltry .262. Meaning, every time you step up to the plate, you have close to a 74 percent chance you'll fail to get a base hit—but you get out

---

6 Nick Baumgardner, "Why This Season Has Been John Beilein's Best Coaching Job at Michigan," *Detroit Free Press*, March 26, 2018, https://www.freep.com/story/sports/college/university-michigan/wolverines/2018/03/26/michigan-basketball-final-four-john-beilein/457539002/

Official statistics for Beilein's career can be found on the University of Michigan website: http://mgoblue.com/staff.aspx?staff=297.

there with confidence to hit all the same.[7] Everyone knows Babe Ruth broke records for home runs, but he had massive numbers of strikeouts as well. When a sports reporter once asked him, "What do you think about when a pitcher strikes you out?" he famously replied, "I'm starting to feel sorry for the next one I face because it's time for another home run." We'd all do well to channel that attitude.

COMMON SENSE GUIDELINES FOR FINANCIAL HEALTH

As much as I encourage creative solutions to financial challenges, the traditional wisdom about money has a lot to offer when it comes to the basics. In the right measure and with the right perspective, you can use the following rules to help yourself achieve abundance.

Achieve a Sensible Balance. To achieve and maintain good financial health, generally speaking, a prudent breakdown of how you spend your money can be outlined as follows:

- Savings (pay yourself first)—10 to 15 percent.

---

7   *The 2006 ESPN Baseball Encyclopedia*, edited by Gary Gillette and Pete Palmer (New York: Sterling Publishing Company, 2006), 5, quoted in Baseball Almanac, accessed April 11, 2019, http://www.baseball-almanac.com/quotes/quowilt.shtml. As Ted Williams said, "Baseball is the only field of endeavor where a man can succeed three times out of ten and be considered a good performer."; "League by League Totals for Batting Average," Baseball Almanac, accessed April 11, 2019, http://www.baseball-almanac.com/hitting/hibavg4.shtml.

- Housing—25 to 35 percent.
- Charitable donations—5 to 10 percent.
- Taxes—25 to 30 percent.
- Lifestyle (food, clothing, utilities, etc.)—25 to 30 percent.

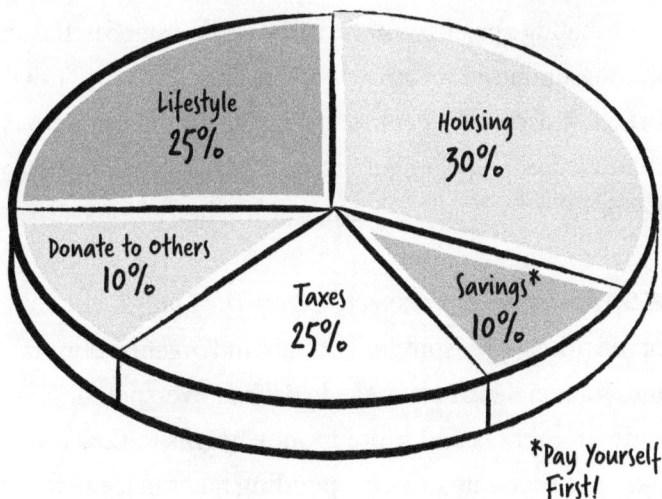

Pay Yourself First. Save a dime of every dollar you make, regardless of your income. This is a concept that very few people apply consistently. I met a woman from Brooklyn who was a multimillionaire in her early fifties even though she never made more than $50,000 a year. I was shocked when she told me she followed a simple rule her mother had taught her: save a dime of every dollar. She did just that, starting with her very first paper route in her teens. Repeating the habit consistently for decades made her rich.

Give Back. Donate a dime of every dollar you make to charity, and give of your time as well. This is part of the ethos of many religions and social movements, and it's not hard to see why. Embracing this practice not only helps others and generates good karma, but also leads to increased happiness for you, the donor and volunteer. Knowing that we are contributing a positive impact to the world around us has an immeasurable effect on our happiness and peace of mind. In fact, most people get more pleasure by giving to others than spending on themselves. Like Maya Angelou said so beautifully, "When you learn, *teach.* When you get, *give.*"

Keep Spending in Perspective over the Long Term. One of the primary reasons individuals and organizations run into financial harm is lifestyle drift or overspending. As time progresses and more money begins to flow into a person's account, a rise in spending takes place without a real understanding of its impact on sustainability.

To be financially bulletproof, you must spend relative to what you have. It doesn't matter whether you have $100,000, $1 million, or $1 billion. People say to me, "I have what I have; when I run out, I'll die." But what do we do if you're still around when you're ninety and you're out of money? I see people underestimating life expectancy all the time.

You need to work mathematically and reverse engineer

the question of what assets you will require to generate a sustainable income. Few people understand that for every $1,000 per month, you would need optimally *$400,000 of assets* to support that spending in perpetuity. That is based on financial and social research suggesting that 2 to 3 percent of accumulated investable assets is the optimal spending rate to sustain an organization or multigenerational family net of tax and inflation. This parallels the endowment mentality whereby many nontaxable institutions set their spending policy at about 4 percent of their assets ongoing for sustainability considering rising costs due to inflation over time. The formula should apply to everyone, but hardly anyone thinks with this endowment mentality.

With these basics of financial literacy under your belt, now we can turn to some useful information about the world of investing.

INVESTMENT 101

Throughout life, you will hear loads of information on investments from simple to complex that can complicate your life. The basic starting principle of investing is to align yourself with a time frame. When will you need to draw on your investments? The process we continued to evolve in determining appropriate investment structure for people is based on their personal vitals to assess

NEED, CAPACITY, and most difficult—WILLINGNESS to take risk. The easiest way to do this today, particularly with young starter investors, is to start with a target date fund, which has been exploding in popularity. For example, you can allocate your investments toward a Vanguard Target Date Fund[8] that matches your expected retirement age. This requires no experience or knowledge, just fortitude to be a disciplined saver and ignore the noise around you. If you can start saving as early as you start earning and get into the habit of saving at least a dime of every dollar you earn, this behavior can lead to tremendous abundance and flexibility throughout your lifetime.

Below is a list and discussion of a variety of investment vehicles and their relative merit.

CASH/T-BILLS

Liquid cash (i.e., money in a savings account) and treasury bills are generally the most stable places to put your money, but are also the lowest yielding assets, meant to maintain liquidity or emergency reserves for the unex-

---

8   Many institutions offer target date funds to scale down volatility and risk as investors age and get closer to retirement. The basic concept is that people upon retiring and needing to spend their money generally have a lower tolerance for handling drawdowns. Vanguard Target Date Fund is just one example of a large institutional provider that may be accessible for individual investors' retirement plans. Many other institutions offer their own versions and philosophical twists of this concept, including BlackRock, T Rowe Price, American Funds, Fidelity, and Dimensional Funds. Vanguard is stated merely as an illustration, and this in no way constitutes investment advice.

pected. It's important to maintain sufficient cash and treasury bills so as to not find yourself in the unenviable position of being forced to sell long-term assets.

BONDS

Bonds are loans made between two parties—whether individuals, corporations, or worldwide governments. These generally yield higher returns than cash, but are subject to more volatility of interest rates. They also have default risks depending on the quality or perceived quality of the bonds worldwide. Most lending around the world is influenced by the United States' ten-year treasury yields, since the default risk of the US government is perceived to be quite low. This is because the US government can always print more money if needed to pay off its obligations. Of course, the potential consequence here is devaluing the currency, but at least you are going to get paid back on your obligation, versus a loan to a friend that you may never get back. The following is a picture of the history of the ten-year treasury yields to give you some context of the history of interest rates for perspective.

10-Year Treasury Constant Maturity Rate

Shaded areas indicate US recession
Source: Board of Governors of the Federal Reserve System (US)

EQUITIES

An equity is an ownership stake in businesses and comes with higher volatility, with the upside that it has the potential to generate the highest return. Over the long term, being an equity owner of businesses has been the source of most of the world's wealth creation. It's worth noting that small equities have even more volatility and historically the highest returns. Larger size, on the other hand, is an impediment to higher returns. It is much easier to double and triple your business by starting from a small size. The Ibbotson graph below shows that, historically, investors in US small stocks achieve even greater success by the numbers. Academic evidence also has become more complex in identifying robust and sustainable factors that can lead to even higher, more persistent returns in financial markets by leaning on small, cheap, profitable companies around the world.

Capital Markets
Ibbotson® SBBI® Historical Growth (1926–2015)

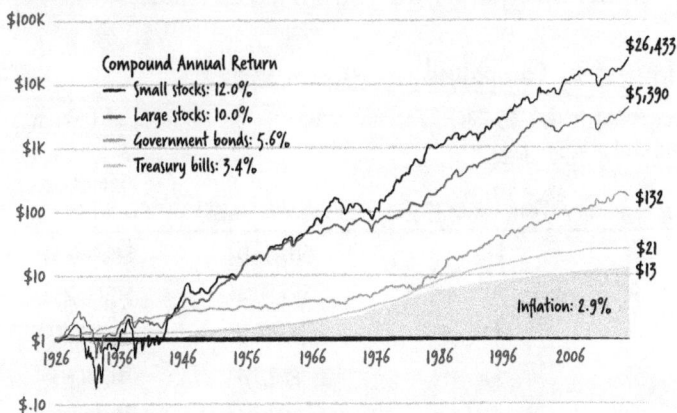

Compound Annual Return
— Small stocks: 12.0%
— Large stocks: 10.0%
-- Government bonds: 5.6%
··· Treasury bills: 3.4%

$26,433
$5,390
$132
$21
$13
Inflation: 2.9%

$100K · $10K · $1K · $100 · $10 · $1 · $.10

1926 · 1936 · 1946 · 1956 · 1966 · 1976 · 1986 · 1996 · 2006

Past performance is no guarantee of future results. Hypothetical value of $1 invested at the beginning of 1926. Assumes reinvestment of income and no transaction costs or taxes. This is for illustrative purposes only and not indicative of any investment. An investment cannot be made directly in an index. © 2016 Morningstar. Reprinted with permission.

It follows that if a person applies this concept while young and saves $5,000 per year in small company stocks, practicing this consistently for decades, then there is a good chance that this person could expect to see significant wealth creation. Of course, the world doesn't quite move in a straight line, so this is more theory than how the real world plays out. The time period during which success is measured will have great impact on your actual experience.

In other words, it is possible to have a ten-year period of time where bonds outperform stocks, which is what occurred at the depths of market declines in 2008. Nonetheless, using simple math, illustrated below is the compound impact of the higher return potential offered over time of the various asset classes highlighted: fixed income, US equities, and US small cap equities.

Impact of Compound Growth on Saving

Effect of saving $5,000/year and compounding annually at historic rates by asset class

# of years	Fixed Income (5.5%)	US Equities (10.1%)	US Small Cap Equities (12.1%)
60	$2,291,451	$17,476,184	$48,068,759
50	$1,303,797	$6,646,286	$15,040,430
40	$725,595	$2,508,661	$4,686,886
30	$387,097	$927,857	$1,441,313
20	$188,930	$323,902	$423,907
10	$72,917	$93,157	$104,977
0	$5,000	$5,000	$5,000

The above table is shown for illustrative and educational purposes only and does not reflect an actual investment experience. Instead, the table merely shows the growth of a savings account where the $5,000 is added at the start of each year, and the sum is grown at the compound rate indicated. Investing, particularly in small cap equities, involves potential loss of principal due to value fluctuations and this is not reflected on the table above. Satovsky Asset Management, LLC does not guarantee that the historic rates of return will persist, not that any particular investing strategy will be successful or profitable.

Once you understand how these different kinds of assets can generally be expected to perform and the risk involved, you can begin to make informed decisions as to how best to position yourself for long-term wealth creation to meet your specific goals.

BEYOND BASIC FINANCIAL LITERACY

The information in this chapter represents my quick financial literacy 101 course. If many of these concepts were new to you, perhaps now you can begin to see that there's much more at play in the world of finance than just the numbers.

To recap, if you save 10 percent of your income, think long term, and align yourself philosophically to an investment structure and ideology that makes sense to you, your probability of success can increase materially. I've lived and breathed these practices on the front lines of the financial landscape for the past twenty-five years and seen them work time and time again—for my clients and for myself.

For the purposes of keeping it simple here, we're skipping more advanced financial planning topics surrounding tax and estate planning and other tricks of the trade. This is because the opportunity set in these areas constantly shifts with changes in regulations and tax policies. Thus, maneuvering these constantly shifting winds, while it can be quite beneficial, falls beyond the scope of a basic financial literacy lesson.

In this chapter, I've also touched on behavioral biases and the (often negative) role they can play in keeping ourselves on track toward our financial goals. I believe that behavioral finance has a greater influence on financial success than the numbers themselves. We'll take a closer look at how this works in the next chapter.

A Formula for Financial Success: Chapter 1 Takeaways

1. Save early and often. Optimally, 10 to 20 percent of every dollar you make should go toward paying yourself first.
2. Invest with a long-term mindset, combining discipline and optimism to stick to your chosen structure during down markets.
3. A simple place to start would be a target date fund. Bundled solutions enable you to spend time elsewhere versus overtinkering with little pieces, which leads to behavioral errors; therefore, consider Vanguard or Dimensional Funds as cost-effective options.
4. Investment in small companies means greater volatility, but also the potential for the highest return.
5. With long-term sustainability in mind, spend less than 2 to 3 percent of your total assets in your retirement years with an endowment mindset.

Chapter Two

A CRASH COURSE IN BEHAVIORAL FINANCE

Only buy something that you'd be perfectly happy to hold if the market shut down for ten years.

WARREN BUFFETT

If you've seen the movie *Groundhog Day*, you might have a sense of what it's like for someone in my position, watching investors make the same avoidable behavioral mistakes time and time again. If you're not familiar with that film, the story follows a hapless weatherman who gets stuck in a time warp in a small town, doomed to live out the same day again and again into perpetuity.

Just like Bill Murray in the movie, every day I witness the same behavioral drama play out on the front lines of the financial planning and investment business. One dramatic example of this from early in my career really sticks out. In the late nineties, booming concentrated technology investment fund Janus Twenty gobbled up the majority of money flows in the world. At that time, investors were abandoning all forms of diversification, value investing, and international investing to pile into the gold rush that was the dot-com period.

Now, if these investors had invested in Janus Twenty in 1996 and held on to it for a full ten years until 2005, they would have close to tripled their money, outpacing the S&P 500 by a 60 percent margin.[9] But in reality, very few people did this. Why is that, you might wonder? The trend we've seen over the past few decades is that investors generally like to test things out. As they get momentum, and a particular investment is working, they buy in more heavily, upping the ante once they feel empowered and confident that they are on the right track. Then, of course, if that momentum turns negative, the masses liquidate in droves.

So, you've got folks buying high and selling low, not exactly a recipe for investing success! That is how it happens, though—rinse, repeat, go broke.

9   Index and fund performance taken from Morningstar [accessed March 2018].

In this chapter, we'll look at some of the factors that play into why the Behavior Gap has become such a prevalent problem in the investment world, along with strategies to combat these influences.

BEATING BEHAVIORAL BIAS

It's my strong belief that behavior and mindset have a greater influence on investor success over a lifetime than whether someone believes in active or passive investing. Look, everyone is active whether they intend to be or not. Decisions are made about money flows daily, weekly, and annually—even if using low-cost index funds—to ascertain how much and whether to invest in US stocks versus foreign stocks, large versus small, growth versus value, and stocks versus bonds versus cash versus real estate versus yet other alternatives.

Since behavioral temptations are going to continue to plague all of us, repeatedly, at any given time, the key to avoiding the Behavior Gap is achieving a core blend of assets an investor is willing to stick with for ten to fifteen years, through both ups *and* downs. That means taking a thoughtfully diversified approach to your investment strategy.

Investor Behavior

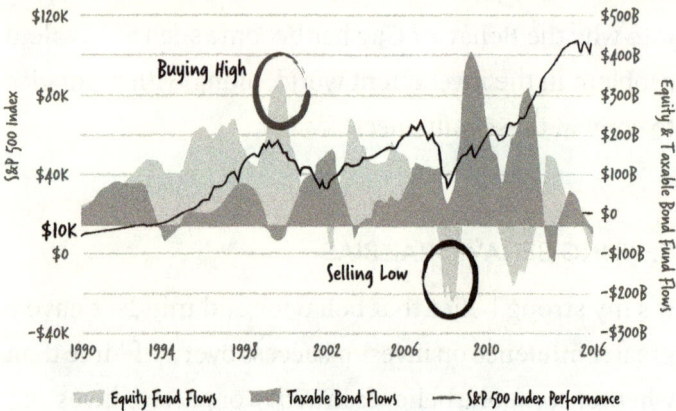

Source: Franklin Templeton Investments. S&P 500 Index data taken from Morningstar, Equity and Bond Fund Flows taken from ICI. Flows are represented by monthly rolling 12-month net new cash flows. Indexes are unmanaged and once cannot invest directly in an index.

In the first decade of the twenty-first century, the S&P 500 experienced two 50 percent declines and returned -0.9 percent annually, scarring a generation of people who were told to invest in the future only to be blindsided by extremely painful losses. I, too, suffered through this period, and while my diversified approach to investing offered some protection, I know if I never go through an event like the period from 2008 to 2009 again it will be too soon.

The reason I have generally steered both myself and those I advise toward a diversified approach is that I have seen time and time again that investors change paths if the portfolios we have constructed experience too much volatility and risk of being out of sync with the world. To further highlight these behavioral risks during extreme periods of volatility, during a decade of the 2000s when the S&P 500 returned -0.9 percent annually, CGM Focus (run by Ken Heebner) generated 17.9 percent annual returns. According to Morningstar, the fund's investors were earning an annual return of -10.8 percent annually—a staggering spread of nearly 30 percentage points. In dollar terms, each dollar invested in the fund at the outset and held through 2009 would have grown to $5.19.[10] The average CGM Focus investor, on the other hand, would have seen that dollar fall to $0.32, or just 6 percent of what the fund ultimately earned. To make further sense of it, investors piled in their money ($2.6 billion inflows) after the fund returns were up 80 percent in 2007—just in time to catch a 48 percent drop in 2008 and subsequently bail on the fund.

Investment Strategy	Holding CGM Focus	Holding S&P 500	Average CGM Focus Investor
10-Year Return of $100K Investment	$518,965	$91,356	$31,890

The above table is shown for illustrative and educational purposes only, illustrating annually compounded historical performance over a 10-year period. Investing in equity funds involves potential loss of principal due to value fluctuations which may not be reflected in the table above. Satovsky Asset Management, LLC does not guarantee that the historic rates of return shown in the table will persist, not that any particular investing strategy will be successful or profitable.

This is just one example of many I've witnessed over the course of my career in which volatility caused people to lose faith and stray from their investment strategy to

---

10   Eleanor Laise, "Best Stock Fund of the Decade: CGM Focus," *The Wall Street Journal*, December 31, 2009, https://www.wsj.com/articles/SB100014240527487048768045746285616 09012716.

chase highs and sell lows. Whether this is driven by fear of losing money, of missing out, or of underperforming benchmarks, peers, neighbors, friends, or family, this behavior is more destructive to long-term investor success than any other single factor.

MANAGING VOLATILITY

Before we get into my own philosophy of seeking the right path for clients who may lean toward lower volatility solutions, first let me give you a test.

If, twenty years ago, I had given you $1 million to invest using one of three investment approaches as your guideline, I wonder which path you would have chosen. Let's say that the time period in question is March 16, 1997, through March 15, 2017.

Here are your three options:

- *Portfolio A*—The Buffett method of investing 90 percent in the S&P 500 and 10 percent in T-bills.
- *Portfolio B*—The "permanent portfolio to weather all seasons" method developed by Harry Browne in the seventies, under which you would allocate 25 percent of your money to T-bills for emergencies, 25 percent in long-bonds for deflation, 25 percent in S&P 500 for

prosperous times, and 25 percent in gold for inflation or economic chaos.

- *Portfolio C*—Jack Bogle's Vanguard portfolio, in which you put 60 percent in the S&P 500 Index and 40 percent in the BarCap Aggregate Bond Index.

Decide which one sounds best to you before continuing. Now I'll illustrate the actual returns for each of these paths. Below is a graphical depiction of the annual returns for the past twenty years of each of these strategies. As you can see by looking at the light grey bars, they illustrate the annual rate of return of the Buffett portfolio—90 percent S&P 500 Index and 10 percent T-Bill portfolio. In 1998 and 1999, this portfolio significantly outperformed the other two portfolios illustrated. However, in the years 2000, 2001, 2002, this portfolio tremendously disappointed investors relative to the other two portfolios, with significant declines in value.

Sample Mindsets

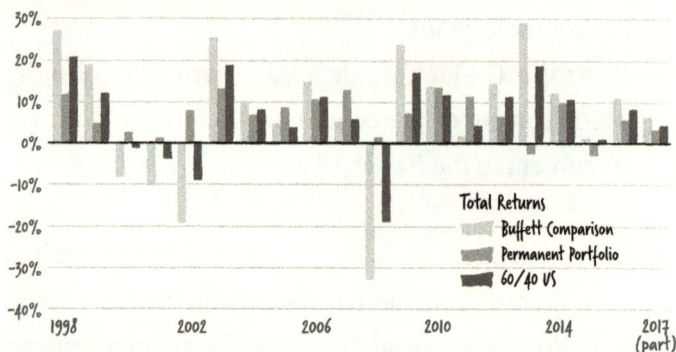

Whether you own Buffett's 90/10, Permanent Portfolio, or a 60/40 Portfolio, it needs to be an ideology that you can stick with for a lifetime. Philosophical alignment is key to long-term sustainable success.

Now you can see why a time frame is so important. The most often asked question in financial advisor offices is this: *What is my investment return this year?* It's a fair enough question—and yet the above graph shows why it's a questionable guide, or even a dangerous one, if your long-term goal is to make money. If you asked this question in your advisor's office each year, you would find reason to be disappointed with any of these paths at different moments in time—thus abandoning either the path or the advisor for a new strategy that appears to be in sync with the world at that moment in time (short-term vantage points blind someone from long-term perspectives).

So which strategy, if held over twenty years, would have produced the most wealth? The answer may surprise you—*all of them!* If you'd passively invested according to any one of these strategies—Buffett's 90 percent S&P 500, 10 percent T-bills, the 60 percent S&P 500, 40 percent BarCap Aggregate Bond Index portfolio, or the permanent portfolio—during these twenty years (ignoring transaction costs and taxes), you would have ended in essentially the same place.

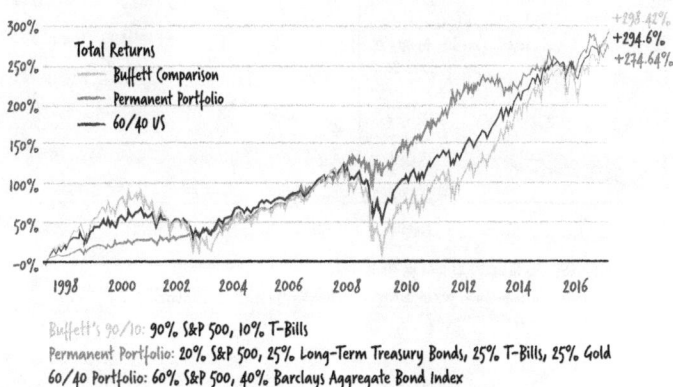

Buffett's 90/10: 90% S&P 500, 10% T-Bills
Permanent Portfolio: 20% S&P 500, 25% Long-Term Treasury Bonds, 25% T-Bills, 25% Gold
60/40 Portfolio: 60% S&P 500, 40% Barclays Aggregate Bond Index

Source: Kwanti Performance Analytics.

Many times during the twenty-year journey, you'd have experienced disappointing results that left you questioning your path, whichever one you took. Would you have held firm? Having sat across the table from many uncomfortable clients, I can tell you that everybody struggles. In my experience and in academic research findings, the emotional reaction to loss creates 2.5 times the response as the pleasure of similar economic gains.

Here is a look at one possible outcome, should you give into short-term fluctuations and impulse. Below, see what happens when an investor alters their path from 90/10 to 60/40 in 2002. The impact to terminal wealth can be quite significant.

Growth of $500K Holding 90/10 Portfolio vs Switching to 60/40

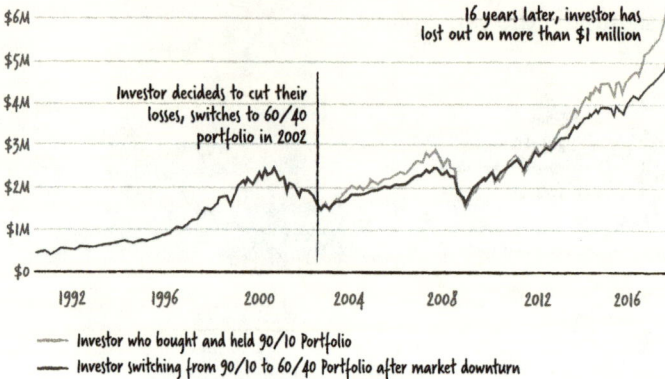

Legend:
- - - - - Investor who bought and held 90/10 Portfolio
———— Investor switching from 90/10 to 60/40 Portfolio after market downturn

Chart annotations:
- Investor decideds to cut their losses, switches to 60/40 portfolio in 2002
- 16 years later, investor has lost out on more than $1 million

Whatever path you choose as you make investments, be prepared to go through periods of being uncomfortable, and to cope with the anxiety of the moment. There will always *appear* to be something better; that doesn't mean it really *is*.

What clients perceive as being high risk at any given moment may be a fantastic opportunity in disguise. The reality is most investors prefer relative returns when the market is rising and absolute returns when the markets are declining. This is human nature and, thus, will likely never change. This means that the phenomenon of the Behavior Gap will almost certainly continue. When it comes to my money and my clients' future, though, I prefer to lean toward the vision for exponentially positive possibilities, as this is simply a healthier way to live.

Staying the course is the surest way to build wealth—but it's not only not easy, it's getting harder. Technology gives us unlimited data and information minute to minute on our smartphones, while the media chases any hint of either disaster or opportunity. These magnets are strong—so developing a Jedi mindset of being unshakeable amidst strong forces becomes a lifelong learning pursuit.

For those of us who aren't yet Jedis—which is basically to say, *all of us*—the key is finding an investment structure that matches your temperament, so that your confidence isn't so quickly shaken during a bad quarter or year. That's my most challenging and exciting job as an advisor: creating the right philosophical blend of assets—mindful of the specific balance sheet and cash flow needs that give my client sufficient peace of mind to sit back and let the market and the strategy do its work for ten-plus years.

Meanwhile, technology, while exacerbating the problem, also provides a partial solution to the Behavior Gap. Modern financial management technology can customize a plan for an individual's specific preferences and temperament in order to mitigate their behavioral biases. In fact, for many clients, we have been using some of the automated investment tools to managing clients' portfolios and saving/spending habits so that we can focus more time on helping them manage their own behavior and on curating the right structure in aggregate.

One automated technology solution we have utilized is on their own quest for Behavioral Gap Zero. By using technology to align portfolios to clients' goals, time frame, and tax efficient investment vehicles, we can provide a behavioral advantage to the individual investor to create higher returns on average over a lifetime. Highlighted research illustrates that market timing and active trading, on average, costs investors up to 6.5 percent per year. By curating the right path and taking the emotions out of the equation, investors and advisors can have a massive advantage over their lifetimes.

Whatever your solution, the ultimate goal is to get out of your own way. Minimize the Behavior Gap, and over time, you'll increase wealth, reduce stress, and move toward the self-sufficiency needed to pursue your dreams. This requires both an abundant mindset and strong planning.

A CONTRIBUTING FACTOR: BAD INFORMATION

I've found that, increasingly, one thing pushing folks to engage in bad behavioral finance is simply bad information put forth by investor peers and, sometimes, even industry professionals and other "trusted" sources. In one particularly glaring example, the May 2017 edition of *Barron's* included an incredibly misleading "Big Money Poll," shown below.

Your Portfolio...

Are you beating the S&P 500 this year?

Professionally	No = 38%	Yes = 62%
Personally	No = 37%	Yes = 63%

Will active portfolio management outperform or underperform investment strategies in the next 12 months?

Underperform = 24%	Outperform = 76%

Here, they asked investors and financial professionals whether they were currently outperforming the S&P 500. A healthy majority said "yes," implying that if you're not expecting to do better, you're a rank underperformer. There's a couple big problems here.

As Warren Buffett's famous bet[11] illustrates, the likelihood of picking an individual or institution in advance

---

11   Long Bets, accessed April 11, 2019, http://longbets.org/362/. Warren Buffett made a public declaration in 2007 stating that he would bet one million dollars that a passive blend of investments would outearn any hedge fund or "active" investor over the next ten years. Protégé Partners took him up on this offer; Berkshire Hathaway, Inc. Shareholder Letters, Berkshire Hathaway, accessed April 11, 2019. http://www.berkshirehathaway.com/letters/2016ltr.pdf. Buffett reinforced his argument in the 2016 Berkshire Hathaway annual shareholder letter.

that will outperform the passive S&P 500 over a ten-year period of time is close to nil. The fact is that active investors hardly *ever* consistently outperform the market over time. What that means is that what the survey *really* tells us is that most people are delusional or are being intentionally dishonest. Perhaps this is the Lake Wobegon effect, a natural tendency to overestimate one's capabilities and see oneself as better than others. Research psychologists refer to this tendency as *self-enhancement bias* and have studied its influence in many domains.

There's a second problem with the poll, almost as frustrating. It establishes a frame that everyone should use the S&P 500 as the benchmark to measure their own portfolio's returns. The S&P 500 represents the five hundred largest publicly traded companies in the United States. Its primary use is to reflect the health of our overall economy. The reality is that people need money at different points in time, and may not have sufficient tolerance for the ups and downs of a 100 percent stock portfolio concentrated in the US market.

The *Barron's* poll is the kind of bad information that, in aggregate, does real damage. People seeing this poll in a "trusted" source may be unduly influenced to alter their investment path. They may be disappointed in their investment structure if they aren't outperforming the S&P 500—meanwhile, mathematically, the claim made by the poll is ridiculous.The SPIVA (S&P Indices Versus Active) management scorecard published by S&P Dow Jones Indices in 2017, for example, reported that 85.08 percent of US large-cap funds underperformed the S&P 500 benchmark over a six-month window. Expand that window to fifteen years, and the number is even higher, at 93.18 percent.[12]

Bad information contributes to the growing Behavior Gap and to the dissatisfaction among investors that prevents them from developing a more patient—and thereby successful—investment strategy.

The solution is to start with honest facts, data, and evidence. A claim that isn't mathematically probable shouldn't serve as a measuring stick. These days, it's incumbent on each of us to be mindful of where we're getting our information from—even when it seems to be coming from a reliable source.

When I see misleading information like the *Barron's* poll, my gut reaction is to double down and scream the wisdom of an index and passive-investment ideology. This is despite the fact that, in seeking to construct portfolios with risk-return characteristics that let my clients sleep at night, I've been fortunate to stumble upon a handful

---

12 "SPIVA US Scorecard," S&P Dow Jones Indices, 2017, https://us.spindices.com/documents/spiva/spiva-us-mid-year-2017.pdf.

of exceptional independent thinkers who have exhibited wonderful upside/downside attributes through a wide range of market conditions during the past twenty-five years. If I can stack the odds in favor of clients, I know that they're more likely to stick with the strategy we've designed.

When considering the health of your portfolio, look beyond the S&P 500 at the big picture. This goes back to where we started: creating a strategy that takes into account your balance sheet, your cash flow needs over time, and your goals. When you deviate from a passive strategy such as a Vanguard S&P 500 index or a target date fund, understand what you own and why it's crucial for your long-term wealth, health, and minimizing behavioral mistakes. You still must be mentally and emotionally prepared for the 40 to 50 percent of the time that your strategy appears to be losing or out of sync on the upside or downside, whether absolutely or relative to your expectations.

THE BERKSHIRE HATHAWAY MODEL

My dream in finance is to create the best possible investor experience for the people I serve and care about. I want to help them create the financial security that frees them to focus their time and energy on whatever brings them joy.

That means managing the behavioral sirens that call to us, enticing us to abandon our long-term strategy in search for something better, hotter, newer. This is a temptation we all face as human beings. After all, we're all striving to be the best and to align ourselves with the best; I know I am.

My goal, then, is to instill greater patience and resilience to promote a long-term investor experience, in order to minimize or simply avoid the behavioral trap. Despite what some say, this remedy has nothing to do with passive versus active investment strategies. It's rather a matter of philosophy, discipline, and understanding.

To highlight the best active manager in the world during the past half-century, look no further than Berkshire Hathaway (which I and many clients own) to remind people of the mindset that investing is a lifelong process. If you have a goal of outperformance over time, be prepared to zig when others are zagging. In active management, it requires the emotional temperament to deviate considerably from the world and be okay with that. It takes Charlie Munger's (Warren Buffett's longtime partner) mindset of indifference to the crowd during periods when your strategy or investments are unpopular or contradictory. (For a healthy dose of Munger wisdom, I highly recommend *Poor Charlie's Almanack: The Wit and Wisdom of Charles T. Munger.*)

Warren Buffett of Berkshire Hathaway is undeniably one of the most successful investors of the past fifty years, and he has generated annualized returns in excess of 19 percent annually for more than fifty years. Below is an illustration of the past two decades of Berkshire Hathaway's celebrated stock performance. But as you can see from these highlights, when investing with Buffett, 40 percent of the time your performance would have lagged the markets (S&P 500) during the past twenty years by magnitudes of up to 40 percent in a single calendar year. In fact, in the past thirty-two years, an investor in Berkshire would have experienced eight periods of underperformance relative to the S&P 500 to the magnitude of 20 percent to 59 percent.

If He Wasn't the Oracle of Omaha, Would You Sit Still?

Berkshire Hathaway has underperformed
40% of the time during the past 20 years

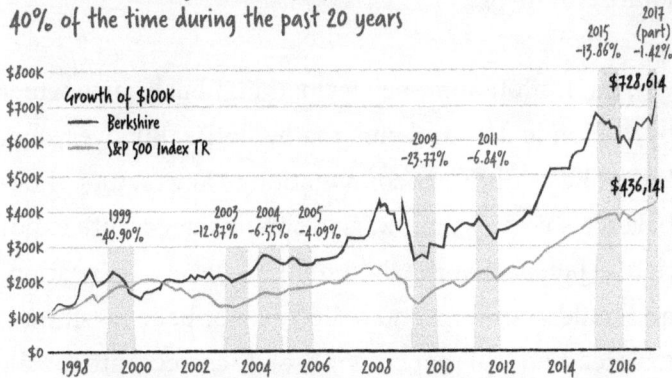

Berkshire Hathaway has underperformed 40% of the time during the past 20 years. Growth of $100K — Berkshire, ···· S&P 500 Index TR. 1999 -40.90%; 2003 -12.87%; 2004 -6.55%; 2005 -4.09%; 2009 -23.77%; 2011 -6.84%; 2015 -13.86%; 2017 (part) -1.42%. Berkshire $728,614; S&P 500 Index TR $436,141.

This illustration shows a real-world example of the power of long-term investing, and also the importance of patience and ignoring the crowd. That said, the question remains: if it weren't for the stellar reputation of Warren Buffett and Berkshire Hathaway, would their investors have had the fortitude to sit still?

For the past several decades, I have been fortunate to advise loyal, patient investors and families who, for the most part, have stayed the course on the path we have set for them even through ups and downs. That's because we've made it our mission to manage volatility in sync with the level of emotional roller coaster we believe an investor can tolerate, with the goal of mitigating behavioral derailments.

Yes, the Buffett approach is unambiguously supported by academic data and pure mathematics. But everyone I meet has a different combination of key factors: their balance sheet, cash flow, age, circumstances, life experience, perspective, goals, ambitions, level of education and understanding, and philosophy or belief system. I have learned that there is no absolute correct path for all, but there is likely a correct path for each person.

We all have different temperaments, and some may only be able to sleep at night with a more all-weather portfolio. They may want to live with less volatility. Warren Buffett, after all, has a massive supply of liquidity and cash to take advantage of dislocations in the world. As of early 2018, Berkshire reportedly had over a $100 billion reserve of cash.

Obviously, most investors don't have anywhere remotely near this level of liquidity to fall back on. As one of my mentors, the value investing legend, Jean-Marie Eveillard, would often say, "Life's bills don't come at market tops." Being on the front lines, poring through people's balance sheets and cash flow statements, I'm all too familiar with the reality of needing cash at inopportune points in time. We work hard to help people strengthen their balance sheets and understand their cash flow so that they are never forced sellers in the market.

Even so, the Behavior Gap continues to be the most persistent issue I see in finance. Only when investors become educated about and accept evidence of the behavioral trap can they prepare themselves to successfully navigate such dangers.

AN EXAMPLE TO LIVE BY

During the late nineties, I was fortunate to stumble upon one of my first financial mentors, the great value investor Jean-Marie Eveillard. Starting in 1979, Jean-Marie helped manage a publicly traded mutual fund, First Eagle Global (originally known as SoGen), based on what he liked to call "organized common sense."

Since the early days of my career through today, I am constantly being pitched on "best" solutions for investments. What I loved about Jean-Marie is that he was frank in admitting that no one could ever truly define best. He'd say, "I have no idea what the future is going to bring, but I have my own money invested alongside you, so if I don't find any attractive securities to own, we'll hold cash. I'd rather lose half my investors than half my money." His position seemed starkly in contrast to all the Wall Street people who were hiring *me* to manage their own investments, prompting the twenty-two-year-old me to wonder why they weren't eating their own cooking. Today, I understand that they were probably just being smart. When it comes to our own money, hiring a steward saves us from blind spots around our own behavior and decreases the possibility of succumbing to emotional responses to the market (aka the Behavior Gap!).

Sure enough, Eveillard's principles proved prescient. In the late nineties, six out of ten investors reportedly bailed on his stewardship as they piled into technology shares, wondering why they should pay someone for underperformance while missing out on the greatest bull market of their lives.[13] (He sat the tech boom out because he believed many stocks were overvalued and wanted to invest with a margin of safety.) Even his own wife called him an idiot during those years, pushing him to buy in. He had a disciplined routine whereby he would spend over half his time thinking and reading (similar to Buffett and Munger), but she wondered how that was actual work and felt he was missing the boat.

Ultimately, he was redeemed when investors in the S&P 500 index lost 50 percent or more of their money between 2000 and 2002. Jean-Marie, meanwhile, generated steady positive returns during those years. And as

---

13   William Green, "The World's Best Investors," *Barron's*, May 30, 2015, https://www.barrons.com/articles/profiling-wall-streets-bright-lights-1432956817.

expected, the investors and money flows came flooding back as investors perceived him to be smart again.

From Jean-Marie and other mentors, I've learned the critical importance of self-discipline, one of the four qualities I mentioned earlier as distinguishing successful investors. I see this as requiring both emotional intelligence and self-awareness, understanding that what's right for you doesn't need to be right for everyone else. It takes incredible self-discipline to be comfortable walking out of sync with the crowd.

Jean-Marie held firm even as his business was shuttering and people were saying, "Why should I pay you to manage my money when I can generate higher returns buying the S&P 500?" And ultimately, he was justly rewarded for having the courage of his convictions and eating his own cooking. His example was incredibly influential in my formative years, offering timeless lessons to apply to any business venture or investing ideology.

Hold cash, ignore benchmarks, buy with a margin of safety, ignore the crowd, and find great partners that share your long-term commitment to investing. These are solid, fundamental principles that can be applied to financial planning for better outcomes and, over time, an increased capacity for staying indifferent to the crowd.

How to Stay the Course: Chapter 2 Takeaways

1. The key to avoiding the Behavior Gap: find a core blend of assets you're willing to stick with for ten to fifteen years, through both ups and downs.

2. If active, be prepared to be uncomfortable when your chosen strategy is out of sync with the market—statistically, about 40+ percent of the time.

3. Staying the course through discomfort requires both emotional intelligence and self-awareness, understanding that what's right for you doesn't need to be right for everyone else.

4. Consider using technology to help protect you from your own behavioral biases so that you can automate and more easily follow Buffett's famous advice to be "fearful when others are greedy, and greedy when others are fearful."

Chapter Three

THE QUEST FOR AN ABUNDANT LIFE

To laugh often and much; to win the respect of intelligent people and the affection of children...to leave the world a better place...to know even one life has breathed easier because you have lived. This is to have succeeded.

RALPH WALDO EMERSON

Humans are emotional animals. We aren't wired to be disciplined. Therefore, it's incumbent on long-term investors to find ways to work around this. These days, we can adopt technology to automate saving, investing, rebalancing, tax loss harvesting, and many of the functions of financial planning and investment firms across the globe. If we can constantly improve these processes, we can free up time, money, and mental capacity to pursue creative passions beyond the world of finance.

But how can we cultivate the mindset we need to buck the Behavior Gap and follow through on our long-term investment plans? As the champion boxer Mike Tyson has said, "Everyone has a plan, until they get punched in the mouth."

BECOME A CURIOUS, LIFELONG LEARNER

Starting when we're young, most of us are constantly being measured and evaluated—whether that be in sport, test scores, or what college we're accepted into. This continues as we get older—what car do we drive, what home do we live in, etc.

Call it the quest to be best. I've absolutely fallen into the camp of the highly competitive, striving to be the best at whatever I do. And when it comes to business, any consultant, client, or prospect wants to know what makes me or my firm special. What are *we* the best at?

But how do you measure *best*? What is the measuring stick?

As we've established, there is no one-size-fits-all approach to finance. For this reason, it's vital to stay curious, to turn off the media, and to start reading and thinking more. People like Charlie Munger and Warren Buffett, two of the most successful and well-respected investment managers alive today, swear by this strategy, as did Jean-Marie Eveillard. They insist on spending quiet time to just sit and think. Buffett has said he spends six hours a day reading.

The benefits of this practice show in the thoughtful strides they've made to achieve incredible freedom and abundance for themselves and their fellow investors. These habits promote continual self-education, reflection, and critical thinking—which in turn lead to independent thought, big vision, and greater long-term success.

Speaking from my own experience, adopting a learner's mindset by design has enabled me to see things much more clearly. With the time I've allotted for study, thought, and reflection, I've made considerable strides digging further into the field of human behavior. And I've used the insights I've gained to help the individuals and institutions my firm is fortunate to serve.

But lifelong learning doesn't even require formal education. The simple winding road of life offers many lessons if we are open and tuned-in to learning.

THE NAGGING VOICE OF NEVER ENOUGH

Once you identify a personal philosophy defining your relationship with money, learn to manage your expectations, and become a curious lifelong learner, you can finally begin to shift your mindset from fear-based scarcity to optimism and abundance. This new perspective will help you create greater freedom, wealth, and happiness in your life in ten, twenty, or thirty years, but also—and perhaps even more importantly—*today*.

Allow me to share a story. In the spring of 2000, my business was thriving and my son was eighteen months old. One particular day, my final appointment for the evening had canceled, and I looked out my office window to see it was a beautiful spring afternoon. For the first time in weeks, the sun was shining and wispy clouds dotted the blue sky.

With two hours suddenly free, I decided to leave work early and walk home through Central Park to go spend some time with my kid.

Back then, my schedule was frenetic, leaving little time to stop and appreciate the small things that make life more meaningful. I remember feeling so invigorated that afternoon by the unexpected gift of time to go outside and stretch my legs, enjoying the fresh air, sunshine, and greenery. And all around me in the park were dozens of other people out doing the same thing—walking their dogs, strolling along, riding bikes. I remember actually thinking, "Wow! This much life happens outside an office in the middle of the afternoon?"

I felt so good walking along that I decided to call my grandparents to see how they were doing. They had a hat-and-glove business, which still exists today, a third-generation business now in our family. My gramps answered and asked how I was doing. "Great," I said. "I had a canceled appointment and now I'm walking through Central Park on my way to spend time with Adam."

Without even pausing to consider his response, Gramps growled out, "It's four o'clock on a Wednesday! Get back to work." And he hung up.

His words stung, but I went home anyway and sat on the floor with my son while he built towers out of blocks. After a while, it was him knocking the towers down as fast as I could build them, and both of us laughing.

All these years later, that afternoon stands out to me as one of my favorite memories of my son at that age. All too soon he was a toddler, then a young boy, a teenager, and now a young man. But the memory of that perfect afternoon we spent together and the sound of his laughter bouncing from the walls of our apartment is timeless, priceless.

The mindset that made that afternoon possible became a habit, one that makes my life better every single day. It makes me a better investor and advisor to others, too.

YOU DESERVE A RICH LIFE

That long ago spring day in New York, I gave myself the gift of abundance. Sure, I could have stayed at the office that afternoon and found some work that needed to be done. But I knew—despite my grandfather's protestations and the powerful social pressure to *go, go, go*—there would be plenty of time later on to do those things. What's more, I went back to work the next day feeling refreshed, rejuvenated, and remarkably less stressed out. This resulted in better focus and higher productivity for the rest of that week and then some.

In 2011, I started meditating, thinking that it might help me move beyond the lingering anxiety of the financial crash. (Even today, I see this negatively affecting investors; at every decline in markets, people extrapolate out to another certain crash to come.) At the time, I was having nightmares thinking about people's terror as their investments declined and the world turned upside down for a while. Indeed, meditating helped me relax and put fluctuations in perspective, i.e., to be greedy when others are fearful, per Buffett. But I was shocked to find that my twenty-minute, twice daily meditation had a second remarkable side effect: to help me break free from a destructive mindset of "never enough."

In our work—and achievement-obsessed culture, it's easy to fall into the trap of feeling like we can never stop working, never stop *doing*—that there is never *enough*. And because my grandfather's generation lived through the deprivations of the Great Depression, I understand where that scarcity mindset comes from. But at some point, we must all realize that when we look at the world this way, we set ourselves up for a lifetime of exhaustion, illness, and unending dissatisfaction with the things we have achieved. We miss the unbelievable abundance and gratitude that comes from being enthusiastically engaged in the present moment.

Meditation helps me get out of that trap, to reprioritize my days in a deep, intuitive way—not just how I balance investments but how I balance the rest of my life. It doesn't make me less ambitious, but it helps me understand what's truly important so that I'm not wasting energy in any sphere. And those days when I think, "I'm too busy to meditate," I remember what the Dalai Lama has said. When his schedule is twice as packed, he doesn't reduce meditation time. He doubles it.

Meditation works for me. You might find other ways to create space in your life for abundance thinking. But remember this: you don't have to earn the right to deserve abundance in your life. This is something we are all born with, though most of us are taught to think otherwise—by our families, our jobs, our culture at large.

Once you begin to think of your resources as truly abundant, that mindset reaches beyond your finances and touches every area of your life. You become empowered to custom design the life you *want* to live and brave enough to seize new opportunities to make that new life a reality. You can put your time and energy into creating enriched and more rewarding experiences for yourself and your loved ones—pursuing your passions, giving time to the causes that matter to you, and courageously moving forward with optimism, joy, and resilience.

An abundant future is yours for the taking. And your first step on that path is the simple decision to overrule those nagging voices in the back of your head that warn of scarcity. You *do* deserve all the abundance that life has to offer.

Don't let anyone—yourself included—tell you differently.

WORDS OF WISDOM FROM THE MASTER

In closing, I'd like to leave you with some words that I

turn to when my clients and I need a reminder of the mindset I aspire to adopt and live every day. No one can argue that Warren Buffett stands as one of the savviest and most successful investors in our history. And so it is that I take comfort in his tremendous optimism about the future. The following excerpt comes from his 2015 shareholder letter.

It's an election year, and candidates can't stop speaking about our country's problems (which, of course, only they can solve). As a result of the negative drumbeat, many Americans now believe that their children will not live as well as they themselves do.

That view is dead wrong: The babies born in America today are the luckiest crop in history.

American GDP per capita is now about $56,000. As I mentioned last year, that—in real terms—is a staggering six times the amount in 1930, the year I was born, a leap far beyond the wildest dreams of my parents or their contemporaries. US citizens are not intrinsically more intelligent today, nor do they work harder than did Americans in 1930. Rather, they work far more efficiently and thereby produce far more. This all-powerful trend is certain to continue. America's economic magic remains alive and well.

If I can help my clients and you, my readers, to adjust your mindset—even just a little—from scarcity to abundance, from the short term to the long term, and to reduce the mental and material clutter that pushes us to make poor decisions about our financial futures, then I believe I'm fulfilling my purpose here on earth.

We live in a capitalistic society where many are on a quest to be best, and value creation is questioned every day. Increasingly, we're asked to exceed expectations at any cost. We're all pushed to "deliver alpha"—in finance, that means delivering excess returns relative to a benchmark. But whatever profession you're in, you experience some version of that pressure. The constant quest for *more* can lead to suffering, both mental and financial, when compounded over a lifetime.

So when it comes to your finances, create an investment strategy that you can live with long term. Then get out of your own way: Automate it and/or turn it over to a financial professional who can act as both steward and coach—whatever it takes to protect yourself from your behavioral biases. If you can't resist exploring, play on the edges so that you don't do any irreparable harm if you deviate too far.

Once your finances are on track, focus on the exponential growth that matters most—that of your own joy, and the joy of people you love. Spend time in nature, unplugged, to get in harmony with yourself and the beauty that is around us, so you can show up more mindful of the impact of your actions on the human condition. At the end of the day, I hope for nothing more than that we each discover and achieve our unique definition of abundance.

The Road to Abundance: Chapter 3 Takeaways

1. Dedicate yourself to continual self-education, reflection, and critical thinking to develop your own definition of best, the formula that will help you build success on your own terms.

2. Embrace an abundance mindset to build wealth and security—today and long term.

3. A quality financial planner serves as both an investment advisor and a behavioral coach; he or she has the expertise to develop an appropriate strategy and the emotional intelligence to help you stay the course.

Chapter Four

EAT YOUR OWN COOKING: THOUGHTS FOR FIDUCIARIES

(AND ANYONE WHO MIGHT HIRE ONE)

It takes twenty years to build a reputation and five minutes to ruin it. If you think about that, you'll do things differently.

WARREN BUFFETT

On April 6, 2016, the US Department of Labor published their final Fiduciary Rule. This regulation's intent is to ensure that clients' interests are put ahead of all other considerations when making investment recommendations on accounts covered under the Employee Retirement Income Security Act. Regarding the initiation of these rules, then President Barack Obama said, "For Americans who are doing the hard work of saving for retirement, let's make sure that they get a fair deal."

This was an essential societal move. Reportedly, over $17 billion per year was lost to bad financial advice, causing a massive gap in financial possibilities for a significant number of Americans.[14] As of June 9, 2017, this law had partially gone into effect, and subsequently, on March 15, 2018, a court decision vacated the rule, which the SEC is now trying to amend or create its own version of.[15]

In light of this or future policy changes, the question I find most important to a financial advisor and clients' perception today is this: how are we to determine what constitutes the best advice? And how can others evaluate what constitutes the best advice for the end consumer in society at large? Is it best to advise investing in the S&P 500 passively and not deviating off this path for a lifetime, as Warren Buffett suggests?

---

14 "The Effects of Conflicted Investment Advice on Retirement Savings," Obama White House Archives, accessed April 11, 2019, https://obamawhitehouse.archives.gov/sites/default/files/docs/cea_coi_report_final.pdf.

15 Brian Menickella, "A Federal Court Decision Slammed the Brakes on DOL's Fiduciary Rule. Now What? " *Forbes*, April 12, 2018, https://www.forbes.com/sites/brianmenickella/2018/04/12/a-federal-court-decision-slammed-the-brakes-on-dols-fiduciary-rule-so-now-what/#7883b39c1996.

This may be wise counsel, but can anyone even do this, behaviorally?

Each unique investor brings different facets to the table—different situations, timelines, temperaments, and philosophies. So, how can advice be measured in the short term if we deviate from the passive path?

In this chapter, I'll explore statistics and evidence and share my view for a solution that I believe is optimal for *most* investors. I will also discuss exceptions to the rules and invite you to make up your own mind.

DO UNTO OTHERS...

Knowing how difficult it is for investors to manage their behavior and to seek sustainable solutions, the first rule in finance and fiduciary oversight should be to eat your own cooking. In other words, only buy for your clients what you would own yourself and what you would buy for your own kids or your mother.

The major quest of my firm is to find ways to improve the investor experience over a lifetime because as can be seen from J.P. Morgan's research shown in the following image, the average investor is making decisions that are far too short-term. Therefore, it's incumbent on those in our profession to work toward turning our clients' focus back to the long view. Otherwise, the chances are that investors will see a fate in the decades ahead like that shown in the graph below.

20-Year Annualized Returns by Asset Class (1997–2016)

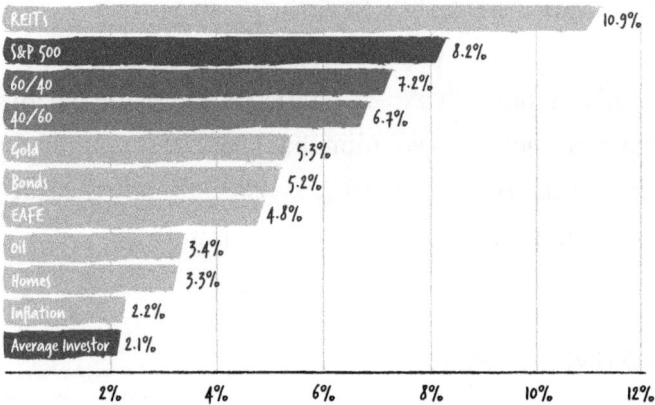

Asset Class	Return
REITs	10.9%
S&P 500	8.2%
60/40	7.2%
40/60	6.7%
Gold	5.3%
Bonds	5.2%
EAFE	4.8%
Oil	3.4%
Homes	3.3%
Inflation	2.2%
Average Investor	2.1%

Source: J.P. Morgan Asset Management; Dalbar Inc. Indexes used are as follows: REITS: NAREIT Equity REIT Index; 60/40: a balanced portfolio with 60% invested in S&P 500 Index and 40% invested in high quality U.S. fixed income, represented by the Barclays U.S. Aggregate Index; Gold: USD/troy oz.; Bonds: Barclays U.S. Aggregate Index; EAFE: MSCI EAFE; Oil: WTI Index; Homes: median sale price of existing single-family homes; Inflation: CPI. The portfolio is rebalanced annually. Average asset allocation investor return is based on an analysis by Dalbar Inc., which utilizes the net of aggregate mutual fund sales, redemptions and exchanges each month as a measure of investor behavior. Returns are annualized (and total return where applicable) and represent the 20-year period ending December 31, 2016, to match Dalbar's most recent analysis. Guide to the Markets – U.S. Data are as of December 31, 2017.

Seeking to avert this kind of outcome is what has led me on the quest for a Behavior Gap of zero. As can be seen in the data above, investors are earning less than they would if they had successfully cultivated the right temperament to buy and hold for a lifetime. This highlights the importance of financial planning and why I'm bullish on the future of advice in the decades ahead.

FINANCIAL ADVICE IN THE TWENTY-FIRST CENTURY

I am concerned the new DOL fiduciary standard, if defended by the US Department of Labor, may lead investors to be too hasty in eliminating underperforming assets for an investor, in the name of fiduciary responsibility. (Indeed, lawsuits are already cropping up against large institutions' lack of fiduciary oversight if they don't replace underperforming investments.) In finance, like in sports, it can often be the case that the underdog or worst performing asset of the last time frame evaluated may turn into the *best* performing asset going forward.

I worry that these regulations may exacerbate the Behavior Gap and impact terminal wealth for investors and advisors. Additionally, in its reporting on the new rules, the press has hyper-focused the public on fees; hence, a massive shift in investor preferences for passive index investments over active investments without acknowledgment of any other relevant factors that may be important to an individual investor—for example, creating a portfolio that allows someone to sleep at night (and hold steady) through both ups and downs. Will it become illegal to express any independent thoughts or opinions for deviating from some benchmark?

The truth is that there is no single right way to go about things. While I philosophically agree with the fiduciary concept—treating others as you would want to be treated means seeking solutions in each individual client's best interest—this rules out a one-size-fits-all solution.

I've come to my own conclusions about what it means for a fiduciary to do best by his or her clients, and how to best serve clients in this new high-tech, tightly regulated environment.

Historically, my firm has sought to align client portfolios to a globally diversified, blended benchmark of stocks and bonds based on Harry Markowitz's Nobel Prize-winning ideology on asset allocation. Put into practice, this is the effort to blend various assets to build an entire portfolio incorporating both higher and lower risk, with the goal of maximizing expected return based on a given level of risk an investor is willing to take. Next, we take it a step further and ascertain if we can find strategies that have exhibited better risk-return characteristics than simple indexes of these asset classes.

What that means for accountability purposes is that every client can measure their portfolios in an absolute and relative fashion comparative to this blended benchmark daily. And even so, every day I see my own clients, prospects, and friends engaging in the same flow of behavior—sending money in after prices rise or when we've experienced outperformance, and selling during periods of stress, during underperformance or losses.

Since the problem of behavioral bias and its financial consequences are rooted in human nature, this problem isn't going anywhere anytime soon. That means that *everyone* needs a behavioral finance coach. This service is worth a premium and will always be of value. Therefore, I seek to help take the emotions out of investing and set a mindset path that someone can adhere to for a lifetime.

Today, technology is freeing my firm to refocus itself on helping clients to manage and make progress on the Behavior Gap, and to work through the emotional and practical issues that comprise an invisible tax on their financial growth. That way, the lion's share of our time and attention can be spent helping clients design—and more importantly, sustain—the investment philosophy that maximizes their personal financial potential.

To illustrate the power of digital portfolio management, I'll share a recent story. We were working with a family with over $100 million in assets spread out across all major financial institutions (Goldman Sachs, J.P. Morgan, Bessemer, AllianceBernstein, and Merrill Lynch). They were invested in a mix of stocks, bonds, mutual funds, hedge funds, venture capital—the best that money could buy. Using technology to organize the information surrounding their existing management, we were able to create an X-ray of the financial health and efficiency of the overall structure. It became clear immediately that cleaning up the management clutter could be executed through technological advancements, saving the client more than $2 million per year in costs while eliminating redundancies, complexity, and streamlining tax efficiencies. One year into the fully implemented new structure, the family would have saved $10 million. Sadly, the client perceived the approach as too pedestrian and opted for expensive clutter and complexity, along with the anxiety and inefficiency of many moving parts.

Meanwhile, my personal vision of fiduciary excellence is unchanged and embodied in these three principles:

1. **Behavioral Awareness: A good advisor builds solutions for the individual, respecting and addressing financial constraints, such as balance sheet and cash flow, but also emotional-behavioral constraints.** This requires a close relationship and significant transparency and trust to allow the advisor to build a holistic solution.

2. **Independence: A good advisor provides unbiased, independent solutions.** In many cases advisors (usually brokers) get paid based on the type and amount of "product" that they sell. This can lead to poorly aligned incentives—cases where advisors have a financial incentive to recommend strategy A over

strategy B, because they receive more in compensation that way, even if it isn't best for the client, or to place more trades in a client's account, because they receive commissions on each trade placed. You even see this in areas like insurance. To an insurance salesman that is paid per policy sold, the answer to every financial problem is to buy insurance. (This is not to say insurance isn't critically important and a valuable part of financial planning, because it certainly is.)

In contrast, we have structured our business and seek to evolve the concept of incentive alignment so that our clients' success and our firm's success are in long-term harmony. Almost all of our fees are currently billed as an annual percentage of assets under our management. This means that as the client's assets grow, our fees grow, and if the client's assets shrink, our fees shrink. This puts us on the same side of the table.

3. **Alignment of Incentives: Good advisors eat their own cooking.** Most of us agree with the concept of "doing unto others that which you would want done to you." So, why invest assets in opportunities—passive or active—that you aren't comfortable with for your own money? When we invest a client's money in an active strategy run by another firm, whether it be Berkshire Hathaway or a mutual fund manager, it is

critically important that we understand whether the manager running the strategy has a vested interest in its success. They need to be eating their own cooking, investing a large portion of their own net worth into their own funds. This shows conviction and helps make sure the client and the manager experience the pleasure and pain alongside each other. Similarly, we make sure that anything we buy for a client, we would buy for ourselves or our own family.

THE HEART OF A SOCIALIST AND MIND OF A CAPITALIST

Clearly, nobody knows "best" and mistakes will be made along the way. But having spent more than a quarter century engrossed in advising others about financial planning and capital allocation and behavioral decisions, I can say this with surety: "The ability to instill long-term optimism in investors is central to helping them delay gratification and stay on course to achieve their financial and life goals."

The principles I learned early on from Warren Buffett, Jean-Marie Eveillard, and other value investors served as significant, formative financial lessons for me. If I can summon even a fraction of their savvy, ingenuity, and resilience to guide my way along the journey, I can do so much to help the people who trust me and my team to keep them out of the fray and on the surest route to wealth.

I have lived through a wide range of professional experiences—from rewarding, to meaningful, to poignant, to sometimes even quite upsetting. What I've often found is that the best solutions come from taking a giant step back from the conventional wisdom or hype of the moment and considering a problem from the roots up. I remember one time a few years back, I was preparing for a television interview on the effects of creating a private social security system.

Fifteen minutes prior to the interview, I was called by the head of public relations at my company at the time. The PR head requested I cancel my appearance, because the company didn't want me to express a viewpoint. I suggested that I had some ideas that were worth sharing without specifically touching on this hot-button topic.

"Okay," I was told. "Just don't use the words, 'security,' 'reform,' or 'privatization.' Good luck!"

Boy, would I need it.

So, I did the TV spot. And after four other people with flip charts and PowerPoints had been interviewed, the newscaster turned to me. "Jon," he said. "Knowing what you know about Social Security privatization proposals, would you have your clients invest in this system?"

"Why don't we consider instead using this as an opportunity to create financial literacy programs in K—12 education," I said, "and mandate it in colleges, so that the next generation is self-sufficient and not dependent on this system whatsoever, thereby empowering people to become financially independent on their own."

The newscaster chastised me for not answering his question.

"But this is the root of the issue, in my opinion," I said.

Perhaps this, then, should be the definition of good fiduciary advice: someone who is willing and able to get to the root of the issue in order to build a healthier, wealthier, and wiser lifetime.

It certainly isn't about mandating the product or solution, since that can't possibly serve everyone's interests. Instead, we need to provide for creativity and flexibility to enable everyone to find their own path in what is defined as appropriate and responsible stewardship for a lifetime of success.

Since I first started in this field, I have worked hard to

understand each person's unique situation and to find the best way to execute on their goals. I became totally focused on finding the path that philosophically matched our clients' mindsets, so that together we could increase the probability of their lifelong success.

To me, that's the difference between financial planning and pure investing. Planners are service people, like social workers, who are trying to understand their clients' challenges holistically and meet them where they are. Investors are focused purely on maximizing returns. I have spent my career trying to bridge the gap and honor both. I often remember what was emphasized to me by a mentor when I started in the profession: "To be successful, you need to have the heart of a socialist and the mind of a capitalist."

Seeking to meet the needs, requests, and risk appetite of clients over their entire lifetimes requires a deep understanding of individual biases. Each investor should be free to choose his or her own adventure, and that means that we too must be free to advise them down that individual path.

Keys to Fiduciary Excellence: Chapter 4 Takeaways

1. The average investor is earning less than they would if they successfully cultivated the right temperament to buy and hold for a lifetime. Everyone needs a behavioral financial coach.

2. New regulations may exacerbate the Behavior Gap and impact terminal wealth for investors and advisors.

3. Fiduciary excellence is embodied in three principles: Behavioral Awareness, Independence, and Alignment of Incentives. Eat your own cooking!

4. The definition of good fiduciary advice: someone who is willing and able to get to the root of the issue in order to build a unique, tailored plan for a healthier, wealthier, and wiser lifetime.

ACKNOWLEDGMENTS

If you want to go fast, go alone. If you want to go far, go together.

AFRICAN PROVERB

Immense thanks are due to the many people who supported me in the writing of this book.

To my oldest child, Adam Jonah—artist and creator of masterpieces which can be seen on adamjonahartist.com and unitedimagination.net. You are a creative, brilliant, independent thinker who enlightens those he meets with music and art, forever challenging traditional thought, particularly my own. You constantly absorb information and incorporate it into your life with speed and discipline unlike anyone I have ever known. And constant reminders that nature, art, and healthy eating are part of the formula to living joyously and with gratitude.

To Julia Rae, my oldest daughter, who's been doing it her own way from the moment she was born. From the time she was little, I've heard, "I'll do it myself." Not only does she do things by herself, often without instruction, she does it all with her own cool style and character. "J-Sat," as her friends call her, you are a rock star in my eyes!

To Aerin Minnie, my youngest daughter, every day you make me smile and laugh, and you inspire me to bring an "enthusiasm unknown to mankind" to life. A blue-eyed card shark, you are hilarious, entertaining, and classy, engaging everyone you meet. It is a blessing to have you in our lives.

To my nuclear and nonnuclear family extensions, forgive me for poking at you in the pages of this book. Know that the lessons I learn from you continue to evolve and develop, showing me more of the positive elements that I seek to extract and embody each and every day.

To James Satovsky, my father, an entrepreneur, scientist, teacher, golfer, competitor, lifelong learner, who is immensely supportive of me in pursuing my passions. You are always there to listen and offer perspective as an eager ear.

To Risha Stern, my mother and editor from day one, your laughter is contagious and brings a positive energy to a room like no other. You fill my whole life with purple hearts, candy, and a zest for living. And of course, thank you for putting your expertise as a former Money magazine guru to work on this book, editing my verbose rambling thoughts into something meaningful.

To Joel Satovsky, my brother, a compassionate, caring, shirt-off-his-back for anyone kind of person who is selfless beyond comprehension.

Immense thanks for the foundational wisdom provided by Charlotte Beyer, who created the Institute of Private Investors to bridge the communication gap between the client and advisory worlds for sustainable stewardship. Additional thanks to the Wharton Private Wealth program, created with Richard Marston, whose teachings about alpha star have inspired my own journey to bridge the gap between investment and investor returns. This foundation has inspired me to be a lifetime learner, continuing to develop a client experience that I have been seeking as a consumer for myself and for my own family throughout my lifetime.

To Warren Buffett and Charlie Munger, the best investing tandem pair in the past fifty years. Thank you for timeless wisdom about thinking and decision-making processes.

Berkshire Hathaway annual letters are a must-read for any business owner or investor, with their brilliant principles and communication during good and bad times.[16]

See particularly a timeless letter about pension obligations that Buffett had written in 1975 to Katharine Graham.[17]

Also see Charlie Munger's speech on the psychology of human misjudgment given to an audience at Harvard University circa June 1995.[18] [19]

To Cynthia and John Hardy, who created an amazing jewelry company, started the Green School, and gave its students a natural, holistic, and student-centered education in one of the most amazing environments on the planet. You have inspired me to spend time and energy seeking to make a positive impact in the world, and helped expand my scope of vision of what is possible with focus, energy, and persistence.

---

16   Berkshire Hathaway, Inc. Shareholder Letters, Berkshire Hathaway, accessed April 10, 2019, http://www.berkshirehathaway.com/letters/letters.html.

17   "Warren Buffett Katharine Graham Letter," Scribd, accessed April 10, 2019, https://www.scribd.com/document/160301289/Warren-Buffett-Katharine-Graham-Letter.

18   Charles T. Munger, "The Psychology of Human Misjudgment," Internet Archive Wayback Machine, accessed April 10, 2019, http://web.archive.org/web/20151004200748/http://law.indiana.edu/instruction/profession/doc/16_1.pdf.

19   "The Psychology of Human Misjudgment—Charlie Munger Full Speech," Recorded circa June 1995, in Cambridge, MA, 1:16:22, https://www.youtube.com/watch?v=pqzcCfUglws&feature=youtu.be.

To Elon Musk of Tesla and SpaceX, who put it all on the line after having achieved great success with PayPal, working passionately to make an impact, dreaming big, learning as you go, and finding passionate support to make the impossible possible.

To Steve Jobs, whose Stanford commencement address is timeless.[20] Connecting dots backward and embracing the journey with passion even through major setbacks that end up opening bigger and better opportunities.

To the comedians who keep me laughing: Chris Rock[21], and Jason Headley[22], whose work speaks the truth.

My SAM Family of the past, present and future, and the myriad supportive, passionate, dedicated people who have worked hard to treat every client as family, only seeking to find diligent thoughtful answers and give advice they would want themselves. You have helped build an unbelievably diverse set of relationships for which we are learning and seeking to make a contribution every day.

---

20 "'You've Got to Find What You Love,' Jobs says," Stanford News, June 14, 2005, https://news.stanford.edu/2005/06/14/jobs-061505/.

21 Chris Rock, "Money Makin' System," YouTube Video, 3:58, September 10, 2007, https://www.youtube.com/watch?v=sY-UXQi4E5c.

22 Jason Headley, "We Are They," YouTube Video, 1:57, April 16, 2014, https://www.youtube.com/watch?v=goVL5dUykzs.

To Sara Grace, for being a kind, compassionate, wise editor who cleans up the clutter.

To Dan Sullivan and the entire Strategic Coach team for encouraging me to both write this book and think exponentially about time, impact, and building a life of your own design.

To the Scribe Media team for helping bring these ideas to life in a beautiful book form.

To Katherine MacKenett, who worked tirelessly with me since I began this book-writing journey in January 2016 to help me find my voice and filter down a lifetime of stories and adventures.

To Margot Ely, former NYU professor, longtime client, and friend, who spent countless hours helping edit and communicate the most salient, impactful themes in an effort to make an impact in the lives of those that read this. And to Joseph McDonald, NYU professor, poet, and educator, for feedback and poetic wisdom.

I stand on the shoulders of teachers, writers, educators, investors, scientists, and mentors from far and wide in learning how to navigate and develop a resilience to keep moving forward and cherishing the present moments. Some favorites include Marcus Aurelius, Paulo Coelho,

Jean-Marie Eveillard, Joel Greenblatt, Steven Romick, Eugene Fama, Jack Bogle, Carl Richards, Dan Ariely, and of course, Jeff Bezos, who lives by the mantra of regret minimization in his own decision-making process.

And most importantly, all my loyal and amazing clients who have entrusted me and my team in stewarding your financial security, retirement dreams, pursuit of entrepreneurship, children's education funds, and planning for multiple generations. I'm immensely grateful and continue to seek out ways to enhance your experience and lighten your load in your own paths for freedom and financial independence.

Never stop learning and sharing lessons on the journey with others.

Live as if you were to die tomorrow—learn as if you were to live forever.

—GANDHI

ABOUT THE AUTHOR

JONATHAN M. SATOVSKY founded Satovsky Asset Management in 2007, which provides advice on over $2 billion in assets and manages more than $700 million. Previously, Jonathan spent over thirteen years at American Express Financial Advisors, joining the Chairman's Advisory Council as one of their youngest top ten advisors.

Jonathan recognizes every client has unique visions, goals, and preferences and offers a custom-tailored approach, aligning advice and portfolio structure to deliver financial peace of mind. He follows industry trends and technology developments, emphasizing continuing education and professional evolution.